Buzz the Bot

by Karra McFarlane

illustrated by Jennifer Naalchigar

OXFORD
UNIVERSITY PRESS

T0369608

Zak gets a big box.

Jen gets a box.

4

Zak gets lots of cups.

Zak gets an egg box.
He taps it on to the leg.

Jen dabs dots.

She dabs a zig zag.

He will be Buzz.

Yes!

Buzz can yap.

He can fizz and chug.

Buzz is quick!

Buzz will not quit. He wins!

Buzz is such a fun bot!